To Yuna, the little pirate in my story.
Susanna Isern

To Yolanda the pirate and Sergio the pirate.
Gómez

ÉGALITÈ

Daniela and History's Women Pirates
Egalité Series

© Text: Susanna Isern, 2022
© Illustrations: Gómez, 2022
© Edition: NubeOcho, 2022
www.nubeocho.com · info@nubeocho.com

Original Title: *Daniela y las mujeres pirata de la historia*
English Translation: Cecilia Ross, 2022

Text Editing: Caroline Dookie, Rebecca Packard

First edition: June, 2023
ISBN: 978-84-19253-60-6
Legal deposit: M-21323-2022

Printed in Portugal.

Daniela and History's Women Pirates

Susanna Isern   Gómez

nubeOCHO

"I've finally found it — my grandmother's book!
She wrote all about the most famous
female pirates in history."

"Did you know that there were lots of female pirates in history?
It wasn't easy being a girl and a pirate back then. You had to be very brave!
(Do you remember how hard Captain Choppylobe made things for me
when I decided to become a pirate?)"

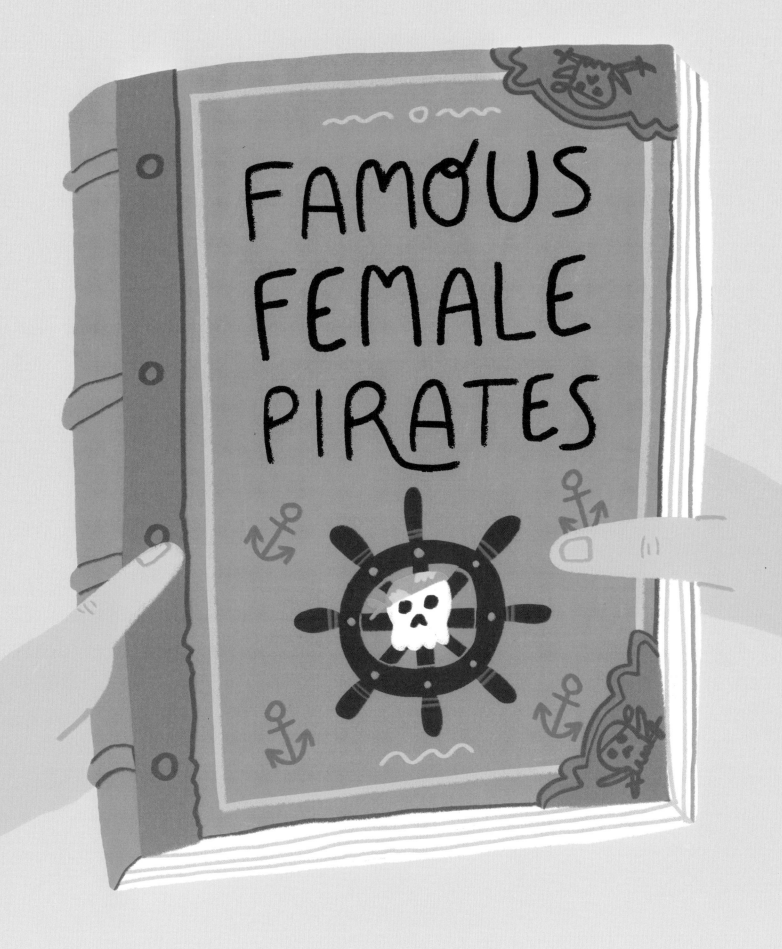

"I'm going to introduce you to these women. They all had such incredible skills, and I've learned something valuable from each one."

ARTEMISIA I OF CARIA

(5TH CENTURY BC) Artemisia was a queen of Caria who helped the Persians in a naval battle against the Greeks. She personally commanded five vessels. She was respected as a great military strategist and was well known for her bravery. She is considered the precursor of all other female pirates to come.

TURKEY

Caria
(present-day Turkey)

The night before the battle, the king of Persia convened his allied leaders, including Artemisia, to seek their advice.

"Let us set sail at dawn and take the Greeks by surprise," suggested one of the chiefs.
"Now is not a good time for a naval battle," Artemisia cautioned. "I propose we wait for more favorable conditions in order to guarantee our success."
"Nonsense! We shall attack by sea, and we will surely be victorious!" insisted another chief.

The Persian king did not heed Artemisia's advice, and at first light, he ordered his fleet to set sail.

Artemisia and her crew fought fiercely. But just as she had predicted, the Greeks quickly began to overwhelm them.

"Queen Artemisia, their ships are getting dangerously close," a soldier told her.
"If they overtake us, we are doomed!" the queen exclaimed. "But I have an idea!"

What inspires me most about Artemisia is her **INTELLIGENCE.**

Artemisia ordered her soldiers to ram directly into another one of their own ships. This confused the Greeks, who thought the attacking boat was one of theirs, so they sailed away, setting their sights elsewhere.

Artemisia smiled and sighed with relief. Her idea had worked. They were no longer in danger.

TEUTA OF ILLYRIA

(3RD CENTURY BC) Teuta was queen of the Ardiaei in Illyria. They called her the Terror of the Adriatic for how she fought against the Romans and because she legalized the practice of piracy in her own kingdom. She was said to be arrogant, unfriendly, and proud.

MONTENEGRO

ALBANIA

Illyria
(present-day Albania)

The people of Illyria were hungry. The land was dry and rocky. Crops weren't growing well, and there was very little livestock, for there was nothing for them to feed on.

"Queen Teuta, our stores of wheat and beans are nearly depleted," the cook told her.
"What about the pigs?" the queen asked.
"There's just two suckling pigs left, and one goat, mostly skin and bones, in the stable."
"If there is no food to be found here on land, we shall seek it at sea," Queen Teuta commanded.

The next morning, Queen Teuta gathered a crew and set out to sea. After just a few hours, they'd caught plenty of fish, but the queen was not satisfied.

"It is not enough," she insisted.

At that moment, she spotted an approaching Roman shipping vessel. It was carrying enough wheat to feed her people for an entire year. Queen Teuta pictured the frail, skinny arms of the boys and girls in her land, and her own son's hungry rumbling belly. She made a decision.

Teuta taught me to **NEVER GIVE UP IN THE FACE OF ADVERSITY.**

"We shall attack the Roman ship! And we shall bring its wheat back to our people, so that they may have bread," ordered the queen.

"Attack!" they all cried.

From then on, Teuta of Illyria's ragged crew became a band of pirates, and she a pirate queen.

Awilda

(5TH CENTURY AD) Awilda was the daughter of a Scandinavian king. She flouted the customs of her day and ran away from home rather than entering into an arranged marriage. She organized a fleet of ships crewed by both women and men, and she eventually became a pirate captain.

NORWAY

SWEDEN

Scandinavia

Synardus, King of the Goths, called his daughter Awilda to him. The time had come to inform her of an important decision.

"You shall marry Prince Alf of Denmark," he told her.
"Father, I do not wish to marry anybody," Awilda replied firmly.
"What you wish is of no importance," the king decreed. "Your fate has been decided."

But Awilda was determined to take her fate into her own hands. She fled, leaving her father and his decree behind, and organized a troop of other young women who were ready to follow her lead.

"Count me in!"

"I'm coming, too!"

"Off to sea we go!"

They set sail on a large ship piloted by Awilda herself.

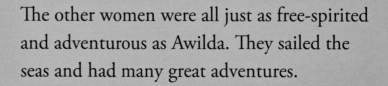

The other women were all just as free-spirited and adventurous as Awilda. They sailed the seas and had many great adventures.

Awilda taught me the importance of CHOOSING MY OWN FATE.

One day, Awilda and her crew crossed paths with a pirate ship.

"Our captain was just killed in battle," one of the pirates lamented.

"Then let us band and become stronger together!" was Awilda's proposal.

The pirates agreed to join the women, and Awilda was named pirate captain shortly after.

JEANNE DE BELLEVILLE

(1300–1359) Jeanne de Belleville was a French noblewoman who turned pirate after the King of France unjustly condemned her husband. She joined forces with the English and was dubbed the Lioness of Brittany. Jeanne commanded three ships that came to be known as the Black Fleet.

CLISSON

France

After the death of her husband, Jeanne and her children decided to rebel against the French.

"Your father may no longer be with us, but we will not give in. We will fight back against the French!" Jeanne declared.

"The English are on our side, and some of the Bretons have said that they're willing to follow us as well," added one of her sons.

"Then it is settled," Jeanne replied. "We will organize a fleet and take to the sea."

With the help of her children, Jeanne assembled three large ships and readied them for battle.

"I want all those who set eyes upon these ships to quake with fear!" she exclaimed.

So Jeanne ordered that the ships be painted black and draped with blood red sails.

It is said that whenever a French crew caught sight of the Black Fleet approaching in the distance, they would instantly flee before it, crying:

"Full about! The Lioness of Brittany is upon us!"

But Jeanne never gave up. With a torch in one hand and a sword in the other, she roared:

"Justice!"

What I like best about Jeanne is that SHE NEVER GAVE IN TO INJUSTICE.

GRACE O'MALLEY

(1530–1603) Grace O'Malley became famous as a pirate and rebel during the reign of Queen Elizabeth I of England. At the age of twenty, she took command of the fleet belonging to her father, an international mercantile trader. She is considered a heroine in Ireland for fighting against British oppression.

IRELAND

UNITED KINGDOM

Ireland

The chief of Clan O'Malley and his men were preparing to set sail for Spain. Grace's eyes sparkled with excitement as she witnessed the preparations.

"Father, I want to join the crew and sail to Spain with you."
"It's too dangerous, Grace. Your long hair could get tangled in the ropes and sails," her father tried to dissuade her.

But his words had quite the opposite effect on Grace. Without thinking twice, she grabbed a special knife called a fish scaler and sat herself down in front of a mirror.

Then one by one, Grace cut off every single lock of that long hair that was standing in the way of her dream.

I admire Grace's **STRENGTH AND COURAGE.**

Then Grace went back to her father and said:

"I am ready to sail now."

And that's how young Grace first set off to sail the seven seas. Years later, she took over command of her father's fleet and became a pirate.

MARY READ

(1690–1721) Mary's mother dressed her as a boy so that she could receive financial support. From then on, Mary became known as "Mark." She joined the army and later became a pirate. She and Anne Bonny were among the few women ever tried for piracy in the 18th century.

IRELAND

UNITED KINGDOM

England

The ship was crewed entirely by men… or so they thought.

The sailor they all knew as Mark was actually Mary Read, who'd earned the respect and admiration of her shipmates due to her incredible fighting skills.

One day during a voyage to the New World, the Dutch ship Mary was traveling on crossed paths with a much more fearsome group.

"Pirates!" Mary shouted, raising the alarm.

But they were unable to repel the attack. The pirates came aboard and quickly took control of the ship.

So Mary decided to become a pirate herself.

Then one day, the lone woman among Mary's new crewmates approached her. Her name was Anne Bonny, and she quickly discovered Mary's secret.

"But you're not a man, you're a woman!" she exclaimed.

Mary sailed throughout the Caribbean, her courage steadfast in the face of many dangers and challenges. She was known far and wide and went down as one of the most famous female pirates in history.

ANNE BONNY

(1698–*c.* 1780) Anne Bonny was an Irish pirate active in the Caribbean Sea in the early 18th century alongside her crewmate and friend Mary Read. When she was a child, her father used to dress her as a boy and call her "Andy."

IRELAND

UNITED KINGDOM

Ireland

When Anne Bonny lived in Nassau (which at the time was known as the Pirate Republic of Nassau), she spent a lot of time in taverns frequented by pirates. It was in one such establishment that she first met Captain Jack Rackham.

"What would you say to joining us, as one of the crew?" Jack offered, for he could tell that she possessed great courage.

Anne smiled and immediately accepted.

Back then, there weren't many women who ventured out to sea, and those who did were almost always servants, washerwomen or cooks.

Only a very few, like Anne, would actually sail the seven seas as true pirates.

Together with Jack and his crew, Anne raided dozens of ships, amassing many valuable treasures.

Anne Bonny taught me the importance of FRIENDSHIP AND OF GIRLS HELPING ONE ANOTHER.

It was on one of these raids that she met Mary Read, who was dressed as a man. When she discovered that she was a woman, she decided to support her.

"I'll speak to Jack, and you can become one of us."

They became fast friends and conquered the Caribbean together.

CHING SHIH

(1775–1844) Ching Shih was a famous Chinese pirate who commanded one of the largest fleets in history, made up of more than two thousand ships and eighty thousand men. She is considered one of the most successful pirates of all time.

MACAO

China

After her husband was killed in a terrible storm, Ching Shih took control of his large fleet of pirate ships. There were so many of them, in fact, that when they all sailed together, the fleet looked more like a giant floating city.

One day, Ching Shih had an idea.

"We need new and better laws to help keep order on our ships."

So Ching Shih created her own code of law:

Absolute obedience and loyalty must be shown to myself and to other fleet leaders.

Villages friendly to pirates shall never be pillaged.

Going ashore without express permission is prohibited.

Stealing from shared treasure stores shall not be tolerated.

Female prisoners shall be respected.

The emperor of China was furious when he learned that there was a woman who wielded so much power, so he sent his armada to attack Ching Shih and her fleet.

Ching Shih made me realize that women make **GREAT COMMANDERS.**

But things didn't go quite how he'd planned. During the battle, the imperial armada lost sixty-three of its ships—because they decided to join Ching Shih's side instead!

"You will have more and better opportunities under my command. Join us!"

Ching Shih's fleet became larger and more powerful.

SADIE FARRELL

(MID 19TH CENTURY) Sadie Farrell was an American woman with Irish roots who led a band of river pirates. She was better known as Sadie the Goat because of her signature fighting move: headbutting. She went from living in the slums to being known as New York's Queen of the Waterfront.

HUDSON RIVER

NEW YORK

United States

One day when Sadie was out for a stroll around the docks, she came across
a gloomy-looking group of men.

"What's eating you fellows?" Sadie asked.

"We're failures," one of them replied. "We tried to take control of that ship there,
but we were bested."

"Well, you probably just need a more organized plan," Sadie assured them. "I'll help you."

The next day, Sadie took charge of the gang.

"Together we'll be unstoppable!" she cried. "Now let's go get 'em!"

Sadie picked out the biggest ship in the harbor and led the charge. Thanks to her quick thinking, this time they successfully took control of the ship.

Sadie taught me how to BE SMART.

Sadie and her men looted boats all up and down the Hudson River for months, raking in huge amounts of riches that they then went on to hide in a variety of secret spots for safekeeping.

And that's how Sadie went from being a lowly street urchin to the Queen of the Waterfront.

LAI CHOI SAN

(EARLY 20TH CENTURY) Lai Choi San, also known by her nickname "Mountain of Wealth" is believed to have commanded a fleet of twelve ships operating in the South China Sea.

MACAO

China

Lai Choi San thought it unfair that some people should have so much wealth while others had to get by on so little.

"The fishermen rise and begin work before dawn, and yet they are still very poor," Lai Choi San was reflecting one day.

"Is there something on your mind, Captain?" one of her pirates enquired.

"I've just had an excellent idea. I've decided that I will help the poor by taking from the rich."

The next day, Lai Choi San sailed her fleet to a nearby town. Once ashore, she paid a visit to all the wealthiest shops.

"To what do I owe the honor of your visit, Lai Choi San?" asked the owner of a fabric shop.

"From now on, you'll need to pay a fee in exchange for our protection," Lai Choi San informed him.

Knowing that he had no choice in the matter, the shopkeeper agreed.

Lai Choi San taught me to HELP THOSE MOST IN NEED.

After collecting several such fees from various businesses around town, Lai Choi San now headed for a group of fishermen.

"Here's a little something to help you and your family," the pirate captain said, handing over a sack full of coins.

From that day forth, Lai Choi San was known as the Robin Hood of the High Seas.

"All of these female pirates have inspired me.
Do you remember the lessons I learned from each
of them along the way?"